THE

SERVANT

CHURCH

Organising Rural Community Care

Elfrida Savigear

Thanks are due to :

- those whose Christian witness in their local community was willingly shared for the wider good.

- the Midshire Caring Trust for their continuing interest and support.

- the Rural Development Commission for their financial assistance.

- the Board of Mission of the General Synod for their support.

- the staff of the Arthur Rank Centre for their advice, hospitality and encouragement.

- the Diocese of Hereford for allowing me the time to complete this project.

- Katrina Terrance for polishing and designing my rough text.

- Chris Bishop for his cartoons.

Published 1996 by   ACORA Publishing,
                       Arthur Rank Centre,
                       National Agricultural Centre,
                       Stoneleigh Park,
                       Warwickshire CV8 2LZ.

ISBN   0 951687I 3 I

Cover design by Chris Bishop.

Printed in England by Royal Agricultural Society of England Services Ltd.

INTRODUCTION

● This booklet sets out to demonstrate good practice to rural churches which are already running, or are thinking of becoming involved in, an organised response to the needs of local people. Such community care schemes can cover a wide range of need. In rural areas in particular the local church might very well be the place where this caring starts. In very small communities not all the recommendations in this booklet need apply, although even informal caring arrangements will benefit from thinking through many of our suggestions.

● Many have asked whether there is a need for a national rural fund. The Midshire Caring Trust invited the Arthur Rank Centre, the Churches Rural Resource Centre, to explore the question. Competitions were organised in 1993 for churches in communities of less than 10,000 population and in 1995 for churches in communities of less than 5000 population. The aim of these competitions was to discover something of the extent of local church involvement in community care. One hundred and fifty projects entered. This publication has drawn on the experience of a sample of these to make recommendations to churches, funders and those who might seek a partnership with the Church in the delivery of care in rural areas. The Midshire Caring Trust, Rural Development Commission and the Board of Mission of the Church of England have each had a financial and advisory involvement with the production of this booklet.

The place of the church in the rural community

● It is well understood that in rural communities Christian activity is as likely to be found hidden within general community programmes of care as in an identifiable church sponsored programme. Accepting this proviso, it is recognised that the Christian Church is one of the main growth points for volunteers and voluntary action. As one of the leading voluntary bodies, the Church needs to be aware of the increased expectation that such voluntary action has to be well organised.

● Changing structures among statutory providers of care and welfare has created a potential contract partnership with voluntary and other providers of care schemes. Such a contractual relationship may involve a legal as well as a financial arrangement. Local schemes such as are common in rural communities could do well to consider whether such a relationship is attractive to help achieve their objectives. But there are obligations too, which may require a higher standard of management. This may in turn suggest talking to neighbouring small schemes to explore the possibility of pooling resources without losing the benefit of local voluntary involvement.

● A community may be defined as a group of people having something in common. In a rural area this will be visible as a hamlet or village, or a more diffuse area covered by a parish council. In the majority of these areas, there is a local church or chapel and this should be a focus for care. Jesus taught us that we should love our neighbours as ourselves. Christians will be aware of the needs of the local community and how scarce are the community care services available to rural people. It is often said that a community is a caring one and yet it is possible for some people to be outside the 'family' or neighbourly net. This may be because their circumstances have changed, or because they feel awkward about asking for help. Many statutory services provide efficient care but this may take a while to establish and local voluntary assistance can be very reassuring for the person concerned. There is no reason why such local assistance cannot be well-organised, aware of legal obligations and of a high standard.

Basic Principles

● Many churches have recognised that they have a Christian duty to care for all members of their community and they have been the initiators of locally organised care schemes. In rural areas there is often only one place of worship. This may include people from several denominations. There may also be people who commute to another denomination nearby. In other localities there are definite denominational groups and these will be recognised by members of the wider community. If one group sets up a community care scheme without the support of the others it gives a confusing message about the Christian faith. Even if sharing in worship proves difficult, sharing in caring is likely to be much easier.

● There are general principles to be followed and much can be learnt from similar schemes elsewhere. Once a vision has become a scheme it is tempting for the service to expand in all directions as individuals point out some other area where care and support is needed. Most schemes that have stood the test of time and are now very impressive began as something small and possibly almost insignificant.

● Clarity of purpose and achievable aims will ensure credibility within the local population, which might be suspicious of a scheme which implies criticism of the locality.

● Most people are unwilling to accept what they perceive as 'charity' and many of the most needy people will struggle to retain their independence if they feel others are doing good to them. Personal dignity must be assured at all times and this may mean organising a care scheme incorporating some form of payment, even if this is at a very nominal rate. Some of the schemes which are completely free have acknowledged that usage was less than expected and have observed that needy clients have struggled alone or sought help elsewhere but when payment has been introduced use of the service has increased. Payment leaves control and dignity with the client.

CONTENTS

TYPES OF SCHEME

Most care schemes have evolved over a period of time and have adapted to the needs of the area. Transport needs in rural areas predominate, especially in the areas where there is no official hospital car service to supplement an infrequent bus service. The schemes studied for this document also covered a wide range of other services :

★ telephone helplines,
★ lunch clubs,
★ day centres,
★ clubs for those with special educational needs,
★ a dry house,
★ bereavement support,
★ help for the unemployed,
★ concern for the homeless,
★ specific projects for one severely disadvantaged member of the community,
★ work with children and young families.

The schemes tended to favour the needs of the older members of the community, but it is important to reflect the needs of the whole population.

Some schemes had clearly defined aims, many of which had been formalised when applying for charitable status or when the scheme was asked to do something which volunteers considered outside their remit.

Listed below are three examples :

'A locally based charity serving the parish.
The scheme is designed to assist in times of domestic emergency
and social need undertaking those tasks not covered by the many
other agencies in the area'.

'To provide help in a crisis on a short-term basis'.

'People caring for people'.

THE CLIENTS

● These are the individuals or groups of people helped by the scheme and they may differ from those for whom the scheme was originally intended. Many schemes encourage clients to become helpers where possible and this should be encouraged as everyone, however disadvantaged, has something to give as well as receive.

● In many situations clients are helped as individuals on a one to one basis and often for one specific request.

● Other situations, such as a lunch club, involve groups of clients where mixing with others is an essential part of the scheme. Any larger group will soon develop its own dynamic and a little extra effort may be needed to assist new members. If clients enjoy the first visit they will usually come again. A personal invitation, perhaps to someone recently bereaved and an introduction to another member, may help overcome barriers.

● Sometimes people have been housebound for so long that they are unable to cope with company, even where physical problems are surmountable. By contrast those who have attended some activity for a while may manage to continue even when exceedingly frail and it may be an important highlight of their week.

One lunch club which has been running for twelve years finds it continues to provide the only weekly break for many of the over 80's. The members have not joined a nearby Day Centre that opened five years ago. An activity that begins at 10.30 am and ends at 3.30 pm may be too long for people who spend most of their time alone and in one place. Personal preparation for a lunch club from 12.30 until 2.00 still takes most of the morning and a client may be quite exhausted by the time s/he reaches home.

Another scheme helps two sisters, both over 90. At first a volunteer did all the shopping. Now the volunteer stays at the house and prepares lunch whilst the more able sister appreciates her greater independence and uses the bus to go to the shops, returning to a hot meal.

Volunteers and housebound clients from one village enjoy monthly outings to places of interest. Over a period of sixteen months numbers have increased from 10 to 22 which is quite beyond expectation.

A community care scheme will only succeed if it serves the needs of its clients. Regular opportunities must be made for the appraisal of the scheme and clients can be actively encouraged to represent the views of those on the receiving end. As a scheme develops this may sometimes need a more formal approach using a follow-up questionnaire or by asking a client to speak at one of the committee meetings.

SETTING UP A SCHEME

There are many different starting points which may lead to a scheme being established. ALL depend upon an individual or a group of individuals reviewing the situation and trying to determine the need. Some successful methods include:

Public Meeting

A meeting is called for all those people with local knowledge such as ministers, health workers, home care assistants, police, doctors, pub landlords, social services, postmen/women and long-established residents.

Village Appraisal

This method of survey can be more successful than a church-only organised survey as all residents are part of the community whereas they may have little or no affiliation with the church. However the church may well have many of the skills required for setting up an appraisal. Church members are often involved in a scheme if the church is not the initiator. The church can take the opportunity to add questions to the questionnaire. Contact the Rural Community Council for advice on village appraisals.

Personal Questionnaires

Two or three in-depth interviews are carried out before drawing up a questionnaire and distributing to a 10% sample as a pilot scheme, amending any questions which cause confusion. It is important to include some choice of questions to allow individuals to describe their own needs and the services they can offer. Common suggestions include transport, shopping, visiting, sitting with a client, and gardening; leave space open for other suggestions.

Deliver the amended questionnaires to every household if possible. There will be a far better response if they are delivered and collected personally.

Personal visiting of households

This method will be the most time consuming, depending on the number of visitors and size of population but it may reveal many needs that would otherwise remain hidden. Information can be obtained from the electoral roll but care must be taken to assure householders that the visit has official support. A note delivered previously can be reassuring.

In one situation personal visits were made to every house and business accompanied by the ex-postmistress. Close attention was paid to the issues being raised on frequent occasions and this detail was helpful in obtaining grants and funding for establishment of the scheme.

Local Knowledge

One key member of the community identifies a need, collects and enthuses others and a scheme materialises. This may be the quickest route and often very effective but care should be taken to ensure the scheme will continue if the leadership changes and that the volunteers do not become a clique. The resultant scheme may be quite specific and this could prevent it expanding to serve other or changing needs in the community. A scheme needs to die naturally if it no longer fulfils a useful function.

One lunch club began on a monthly basis many years ago when a daughter was concerned for her housebound mother who was becoming increasingly lonely and depressed. Discussions with a social worker revealed this as a widespread problem. Now the club runs weekly and provides meals for twenty-five people.

VOLUNTEERS

a) Recruitment and Selection

● Most successful schemes will be used more and more once they become established and there will be a continual turnover of volunteers although this may be slow. If the scheme has a high profile it will probably attract volunteers without too much effort but it is essential that there is a policy for recruitment and selection. Long-established residents may be willing to assist with a scheme once they have seen what is involved. Many of the newcomers attracted to rural areas frequently want to involve themselves within the community. Personal contact and invitation seems to produce the most suitable and committed volunteers. It is a frequent comment that everyone knows everyone in a rural situation but however small the scheme it is essential to be able to select volunteers.

● Most people can think of one local person who would be unsuitable as a volunteer, so there must be a strategy to deal with such a person if s/he were to apply. This is an especially sensitive issue in a close-knit rural community. Other local charities may be able to offer them something more suitable.

● A form (see example on page 8) for collecting the basic factual information can include extra questions relevant to specific tasks. It is advisable to ask about prosecutions / criminal offences and if this is a routine question to all it is unlikely to cause offence. Involve two people in a selection chat or interview. At least one reliable reference should be requested and kept. Committee members may act as referees but this should be clearly recorded with the selection material. It is worth having a list of questions which each volunteer is asked so that personal questions which may appear of a discriminatory nature are avoided. Such procedure would be a minimum for any equivalent statutory position and it is required for the protection of the client, volunteer and the good name of the scheme. Volunteers are unlikely to object to a formal procedure as it shows the scheme is concerned with safety. The casual approach may seem less threatening but would be difficult to justify if there were any problems at a later date.

● Police checks are required for those who work with children and it may be possible to get assistance with this from the Department of Social Services. You may wish to ask some volunteers to apply for this on their own behalf (the information is subject to the Data Protection Act). This will cost £10, and should be paid for by the scheme.

● Identity cards may seem an unnecessary formality but they provide reassurance and security for both volunteer and client. It is unfair to assume that a well-known local person is known by all. Police advise householders to check the credentials of all visitors, especially those who will enter the house or provide lifts. Most schemes try to link a volunteer with a client so that trust builds up but on occasions it will be necessary to use someone different.

● Schemes may have their own Code of Practice or constitution which they could require a new volunteer to sign confirming that they are happy to work within the guidelines. Many of the schemes set up by churches identify their work in accordance with Christian belief and request volunteers to be in sympathy with the same.

Sample Volunteer Form

I wish to become a volunteer for .... Servant Church

NAME ....

ADDRESS ....

Tel. No. .... Date of Birth (for insurance) ....

Area(s) I wish to help with :   TELEPHONE   BEFRIENDING

   PRACTICAL   TRANSPORT

Relevant experience or interests :

Times available during the week :

Complete either A or B

(A)   I attend church or chapel regularly   YES   NO

(B)   I am in sympathy with the Christian faith on which the scheme is based
       and am willing to support these beliefs in any work I do for it.

             Signed.. Date........................

Please give details of any criminal convictions.

Name and address of someone willing to support your application :
(eg. minister, employer . . . .)

NAME   NAME
POSITION   POSITION
ADDRESS   ADDRESS

CODE   CODE
Tel.   Tel.

b) Supervision

● Community care schemes are likely to work with clients who are in a more vulnerable situation than other members of society. If one helps a neighbour purely as a friend it is embarrassing if something goes wrong; but where that help is offered by an organised scheme it is of paramount importance that the service provided is beyond reproach. The word supervision may sound threatening to a volunteer but it is essential to have some system for monitoring the service given so that any problems involving either client or volunteer are easily resolved as part of a recognised routine. Oversight will provide essential support when needed and is not intended to inhibit the individual's style of care. In many situations the coordinator is in regular contact with volunteers. It should be part of the routine to inquire whether there are any problems or concerns which need resolution.

● Sometimes an issue may seem of such a trivial nature that volunteers find it hard to raise, or they may wish to remain anonymous. This can be approached in a variety of ways but a suggestion / problem box could be available (which clearly accepts anonymous queries) and every so often it may be advisable to raise issues in a meeting open to all concerned. It is important to remember that personality clashes occur between the most saintly people and in every situation there should be the opportunity for any individual to speak to someone else about a problem. This may be best achieved by having the support of a 'friend' of the organisation who can reflect on the situation from a dispassionate point of view.

Supporting one another

● Within small groups volunteers will support one another but in larger schemes it should be possible to develop support groups for those involved in a similar type of caring. Cross-scheme support groups linking carers from other nearby communities will provide support and new insights. Regular meetings of those who are befrienders, for example, will be supportive and any difficulties or worries can be discussed. A newsletter will remind volunteers that they are an important member of a team and can be used to pass on supportive information of a general nature. A social activity, such as a barbecue or a Christmas party, can be used to show appreciation of volunteers and this may be all that is needed.

> One lunch club invites all the volunteer drivers to join the clients for the Christmas meal and this is probably the only time the drivers meet together. It is a wonderful opportunity for saying 'thank you'.

c) Training

● Schemes often run their own training sessions, such as an evening on listening skills, safe lifting or basic first aid. Where this is used alongside a business meeting there is often a more enthusiastic attendance. This may also be a useful technique to persuade volunteers of the benefits of other courses, especially where they may be unsure of their own capabilities.

> A club for forty people with learning difficulties invites volunteers to talks on relevant topics such as aggression, sexuality, acceptable and unacceptable behaviour, epilepsy etc.

● Volunteers of all ages and experience will benefit from training and many will gain much personal satisfaction from attending courses especially if they are directly applicable to the scheme. If volunteers can be encouraged to attend as a group this can be of social importance and provide a natural network for support. Some qualifications will be of use to the volunteer in other situations and this may be a useful 'carrot' if there seems to be any reticence about attendance. Courses may be run by a local college or by private or charitable organisations such as Relate. The scheme must be prepared to finance training and certification, although some volunteers may wish to pay for themselves. Some charities are educationally orientated and they may be worth approaching for financial help.

> One volunteer assisting with the Church Welfare Project joined a Debt counselling programme organised by the Mothers' Union. After working with the scheme for some time he undertook further training and became a full-time social worker.

Useful additional reading.

"Volunteers in Community Care", Ann Meadows pp 14-18
Hereford and Worcester Community Council 1996, ISBN 1 873281 05 6

Resource Pack for Voluntary Care Groups, Portsmouth Diocesan CSR 1994 £10

ORGANISATION

● If a scheme is needed and of value it must be accountable to the community it serves. It needs a committee with someone to take the chair, a secretary and a treasurer. For a small scheme the number of meetings may be minimal and they may be quite informal, but accurate records should be kept both of services requested and volunteer usage. The treasurer must be able to supply details of income and outgoings and the accounts should be checked by a second person.

> One helpline scheme uses a hardback desk diary to record all services undertaken and the volunteers used. It can easily be referred to during the year and past copies are kept as a permanent record.

● As a scheme grows it may need to formalise and expand its method of organisation (i) and may require more committee members and sub-groups to deal with the different aspects of the scheme. When more people are involved in the organisation of a scheme it is less likely to become a clique. Voluntary organisations frequently have difficulty in recruiting committee members because too much is demanded from too few individuals. Care should be taken when identifying the tasks. Job-sharing may greatly reduce the burden, whilst also providing cover for holidays and emergencies. Some appointments could be for a fixed term, such as three years, which might help recruitment. On occasions it may be worth coopting additional members of the community to represent one specific interest or to act in an advisory role.

(i)   See Chapter 3, Good Neighbours, David Clark, (Joseph Rowntree, 1991), ISBN 1872470 48 3.

INFORMATION AND CONFIDENTIALITY

● Some information is readily available by means of the electoral register or telephone directory. These can be useful to check addresses where handwriting is unclear. It is worth contacting the library service for details of the local census data as this often yields some surprising information about a population and may identify an area of need which is hidden from the surface. Such information may be a useful tool when applying for grants or funds. For established schemes it is important to monitor the progress of the scheme because, as the needs of the community change, so the nature of the scheme may need to change too.

● In several of the Church of England dioceses the Council for Social Responsibility has obtained the census information and broken it down to individual parish level. It is available to those who request it.

● Rural areas are well known for gossip. However it is often the gossip which stimulates much of the essential neighbourly care. When a more formal scheme is suggested residents fear it will be an opportunity for increased nosiness and great care will be needed to alleviate this fear. Volunteers may have access to very personal information about individuals and they must be reminded frequently that this is confidential. If a volunteer is concerned in any way about an individual client there must be a clear policy of disclosure which will keep those involved to a minimum.

> From one scheme's guide to volunteers : Confidentiality is very important and any information given by a client must be kept to oneself. If it is necessary to share a problem with a team member, permission should first be sought from the client.

● For some of the larger schemes it is possible for volunteers to retain some privacy, such as no access to their private telephone numbers. This can allow for a greater freedom to all parties.

● On occasions it may be important for the client and volunteer to meet on neutral ground and use can be made of a quiet café or some similar venue. It is only the larger schemes which may be able to offer anonymity. There are situations where an outsider can be more objective than a family member who is emotionally involved.

RELATIONSHIP WITH THE CHURCH

■ It is well understood that Christians are likely to express their compassion in whatever scheme of help is organised, whether secular or sponsored by the local faith community. We recommend that the worshipping community should recognise and affirm the caring that takes place in the community, whether or not it is a church scheme. The recommendations below are addressed particularly to churches which have initiated their own scheme.

■ Local churches should receive reports on the scheme at least once a year preferably at an open meeting.

■ The scheme should ask to be recognised annually in a church service (maybe on the anniversary of the scheme).

■ There should be regular prayer for the scheme remembering the volunteers, the coordinators / leaders, and the clients.

■ The church leadership should provide support for the coordinators / leaders and, when requested, pastoral support for the clients.

■ A member of each church leadership team should be assigned as a special 'link' person.

■ The scheme should be mentioned within sermons and teaching whenever applicable as local examples of living the Christian life.

■ Thanks should be given to those involved in the scheme, informally and personally, but also formally by letter, in the church magazine, newsletter etc.

■ Many schemes felt support decreased when there was a change in church leadership - both sides need to recognise that this is a common weakness; both need to make an effort to inform and include the other within general church policy.

■ The scheme should where possible be recognised more widely by inclusion on a Diocesan or Circuit Prayer calendar for example.

■ Local 'Churches Together' groups are flourishing where Christians are working together in a care scheme. Denominational differences seem less important and ecumenical church services have become more joyful and united.

How one church celebrates a community that cares

Reading St John 15:11 - 17 or Matthew 25:31 - 40.

Members of the scheme present items representative of the work they do.

THEY SAY TOGETHER :
We present these gifts as tokens of our desire to serve our world in caring for others, so that we may perceive the need and offer ourselves in service and friendship for the relief of suffering and pain.

MINISTER :
We thank you for the work you do on our behalf.
May your purposes be fulfilled. Help us to be ready to share in your caring and giving, so that we also may assist in creating new lives for those in need.
Receive this light (*a lighted candle may be given*) as a sign of your vision for the future. May it guide you in the ways of peace and justice and the care of those in need.

A REPRESENTATIVE RECEIVES THE CANDLE AND REPLIES :
Jesus, friend of the friendless, helper of the poor, healer of the sick, whose life was spent doing God's will, let us follow in your footsteps. Make us loving in all our words and all our deeds; make us strong to do right, gentle with the weak, and kind to all who are in sorrow, that we may be like You, our Lord and Master. Amen.

MINISTER :
As one Christian body, let us therefore pledge ourselves anew to the service of God and of everyone, that we may help, encourage and comfort others, and support those working for the relief of the needy and for the peace and welfare of our society.

ALL :
Lord God our Father, we pledge ourselves to serve You and everyone in the cause of peace, for the relief of want and suffering and for the praise of your name. Guide us by your spirit; give us wisdom; give us courage; give us hope; and keep us faithful now and always.
Amen.

INSURANCE

● Many schemes assume that because they are working in a neighbourly way they can be casual in their attitudes. It cannot be stressed too strongly that an organisation, however small, has an obligation to those people who act as volunteers and to those people who request help. Insurance is complicated but needs to be considered carefully, as one accident could so damage the reputation of the scheme that it never recovers . The repercussions may seriously affect the close-knit rural community. Schemes which involve use of private cars should check their drivers are covered for whatever journeys they may carry out. It is helpful to have a standard letter available for the volunteer to send to their insurance company. Public liability and protection of a driver's no claims bonus should be the responsibility of the local scheme. The insurance premium may be high for such insurance as most companies have a minimum premium. It is worth contacting other local charities to see if it is possible to be part of a group policy.

● Some schemes offer help and a client may push for advice. This should never be given without a disclaimer, but some policy may be necessary to protect the volunteer and scheme if material of an advisory nature is often requested.

> The Council for Social Responsibility representing three dioceses of the Church of England has obtained a group insurance policy covering the needs of care schemes. This is a great help to the smaller schemes where there is a shortage of funds.

● Insurance of buildings and equipment should be checked but in all these cases it is advisable to see if there is any other insurance under which the scheme would already be covered. Alternatively it may be possible to have the scheme formally adopted under some other body, such as the Parish or church council. This may result in a lower premium or even no extra costs.

EMERGENCIES

● Every scheme should have a clearly developed emergency routine which recognises that, while every member will do their best, sometimes things go wrong. Where the scheme involves use of some building other than the volunteer's home it should be adequately heated; personal safety and security of the volunteer should be top priority.

● When a large group of volunteers or clients meet together, as they might do for a lunch club, other considerations should be made. The building should have been visited by a Fire Officer who will give advice on safety, especially emergency exits. All volunteers need to be acquainted with the emergency routine and regular practices are advisable. One volunteer could be given the responsibility to check that standards do not slip (such as blocking exits with tables). If there is no phone on site, such as in many church halls, loan of a mobile phone could provide peace of mind and may be a lifeline if the emergency services are needed.

First Aid

● The First Aid Box should be clearly on display and checked regularly. Volunteers who are qualified first aiders should be identified and all volunteers should be asked to attend a simple first aid talk. Contact should be made with the local Red Cross or St John's Ambulance group and volunteers encouraged to take further training.

One Kids' Club even found it necessary to have two first aid kits; one to satisfy the requirements of Social Services and one following the recommendations of the organisations who provide the training and certification of First Aiders.

THE TELEPHONE

● Requests for help are most commonly received by telephone and each scheme has to find the most satisfactory way of organising requests. It is advantageous, where possible, to have a single telephone number which can be well advertised and clearly visible on all publicity material. Some well-tried methods are listed below:-

■ One telephone number at an office where personal contact can be made during advertised hours and messages left on an answerphone for the remainder of the time.

■ One telephone number is used and calls are transferred to the person 'on duty'. (Cost about £7.00 per quarter, plus the local call rate.)

■ One telephone number is used linked to an answerphone. The message is changed to give the telephone number of the person 'on call' at the time. The person requesting help has to make two calls but gets a personal response to the second call. A set of clearly labelled individual tapes for each volunteer will aid administration.

■ Several telephone numbers are listed, with each person taking responsibility for general duties. If no answer is obtained from the first call the client tries another number. It is inadvisable to list numbers vertically as the first person on the list will tend to receive the most calls! Printing the numbers in a circle as 'spokes' of a wheel will produce a more even load.

■ Several telephone numbers are listed; each related to a particular area of need such as transport. This can put a tremendous burden on individuals who may feel guilty if they are not available 24 hours a day!

● Publicity is of paramount importance and the number(s) need to be well advertised, so that when a need arises the service can be used. Small brightly coloured stickers to attach to the home telephone might be effective, or a small card to keep near the phone.

> One transport coordinator is disabled herself, but she is willing to receive all the telephone enquiries and organises an appropriate driver when a lift is requested.

TRANSPORT

✗ All drivers should record mileage and be reimbursed at a known rate. Some drivers may wish to donate this money to the scheme if they find receiving money embarrassing.

✗ A letter for volunteers to send to their car insurance firms is useful, providing full details of the scheme so individual drivers get confirmation of cover.

✗ A group insurance to cover volunteers for public liability and personal accident is worthwhile. It is also advisable to protect individual drivers against loss of any no claims bonus.

✗ Each driver should have some form of identity disc for the car which can be used at hospital car parks. Most hospitals will not charge volunteer drivers for parking when on official duty but a formal request for exemption should be made.

> One scheme provides the volunteer driver with a large magnetic rubber panel to fix on the outside of the vehicle. This advertises the scheme and also acts as an identification which prevents charging or clamping at hospital car parks.

✗ Transport coordinators should try and use ALL volunteers and avoid over-usage. This may mean extra phone-calls to arrange a driver. Ideally no volunteer driver should be used more than once a week but some individuals may be very willing to do much more.

✗ Some commuters may now be extremely useful as volunteers following increased use of day surgery, where a patient may need to be at a clinic by 8.00 or 8.30 am. These drivers may be unaware how useful their contribution could be.

✗ Costs for well-used routes such as those to distant hospitals should be advertised at a standard rate as most clients will find this helpful. If there are financial problems this can be waived; where clients choose to donate more money it should be put into general funds.

✘ Drivers should keep a record of the money they receive and details should regularly be passed to the treasurer so that adjustments can be made where necessary. When social services are funding the journey a receipt system will be required.

✘ The scheme insurance policy may specify an age limit for cover for drivers (usually 70). Many schemes are dependent upon older drivers so some policy decision will have to be made. Drivers could be required to have an annual medical check and accept responsibility for personal liability.

CATERING

- Health and hygiene regulations apply to any situation involving storage or preparation of food where it is outside the normal home situation. Some of the rules seem bewildering and excessive for a small organisation, but most local Environmental Health Officers (EHO) want to encourage and assist voluntary schemes and will give helpful advice rather than condemn genuine efforts which are so important to the local community. Where a new club is being planned it is advisable to ask advice from the local EHO at an early stage as the scheme may have insufficient finance to update the facilities and equipment if this is seriously below standard. Occasionally up and running schemes will find they are unable to satisfy the latest legislation, particularly if they are using rented accommodation, but there may be different ways of providing an excellent hot meal.

Methods which have proved satisfactory include :-

- Local pubs/hotels can be asked to quote for producing the meals, remembering that this will be supporting local business by providing a regular income often at a time when business is slack. Be careful to allow all local businesses to tender for the work and when a contract is drawn up ensure that it allows for a probationary period.

- Some school kitchens and those providing meals on wheels have facilities for producing larger numbers of meals than they need themselves and as such services are normally out to tender many will offer a very competitively priced option. School holidays may not be a problem, as meals can be prepared and frozen when there is a full staff working, then produced as required using minimal staff. Some clubs find they get more food in the holidays as portions have been frozen in multiples of seven!

- Some local residential homes/nursing homes would also value the opportunity to tender for provision of meals and many of these are also willing to provide 'hot-box' meals to be delivered to the housebound.

One flourishing club originated with a simple fish and chip meal purchased locally and washed down with a cup of tea. This demonstrated the importance of the social aspect of a club and is a reminder that many clients will be satisfied by a simple meal. Volunteers are also able to spend more time with the clients and less time in planning, purchasing, preparing and cooking.

Self-Catering

● The person in charge of the catering may need to have a hygiene certificate. All volunteers should be encouraged to take the training and obtain the certificate. A successful lunch club should be able to pay one supervisor and this may assist in gaining acceptability with the public authorities. Many groups thrive on individual teams having their own choice of menu and division of labour. Care must be taken to avoid stifling this enthusiasm. However, it is easy for a small group to be overwhelmed with a job they took on several years ago and which no-one else will now take on. This is when a recognised supervisor may be able to assume much of the onerous work and new volunteers may then be more willing to offer their services.

● Food may be prepared at home and brought to the central kitchen for cooking, or transported ready cooked PROVIDED all the safety precautions are followed and hot food is not allowed to drop below a temperature of 63°C.

One lunch club has a very successful arrangement with the local probation service whereby the club pays for the food but the food purchase, preparation, serving and clearing up is carried out by a team of three or four supervised by a member of the probation team. The service is excellent and both sides benefit from the arrangement. The club officials can concentrate on membership details and social aspects and no-one is left outside in the kitchen. The probation service also provides and washes the laundry and other equipment.

Venue

● Food always tastes better in a pleasant environment and any extra effort involved helps the clients to feel they are valued. The room should be warm, clean and safe and the furniture suited to the needs of the clients. Many clubs find someone is willing to be responsible for the table cloths, decorations etc. relieving other volunteers to help with serving and clearing up duties.

MONEY

● Normally schemes need money so that they are able to meet a volunteer's expenses. Some schemes pride themselves on providing a good service and surviving with little or no funds. This is only possible because volunteers do not charge for their time but many of them give other things also, such as not charging for telephone calls. The volunteers would identify this as part of their personal charitable giving and many would find it easier not to complete personal claim forms for relatively small amounts. Others may be prevented from volunteering if they feel they are expected to subsidise the service.

● Once a scheme has over £1,000 annual income, it may be necessary to register as a charity. This will demand an acceptable constitution and may involve some specialist assistance. There are advantages in formal recognition, as charities and grant-giving bodies always require evidence of good practice. Many organisations find that once they become eligible for one source of finance other grants are available too. When requesting financial aid a clear record of previous expenditure will be requested so it is advisable to keep accurate records from the start as they can be used in monitoring effectiveness and the true cost of a scheme. The Rural Community Council can advise on these questions.

● Parish and District Councils have direct concern for a local community and will often provide funding for a scheme. They will require some financial history and may expect a new application annually as a means of assessing the use of their grant. If finance is not required every year it may be advisable to retain friendly but formal contact by means of a letter. Gifts of equipment such as a cooker or an answerphone, or gifts in the form of assistance such as printing or photocopying should be encouraged. Many local businesses will be more generous than with a direct financial gift and appreciate the publicity which can be associated with a specific item.

A local garage donated an answerphone which helps the transport coordinator of one scheme.

Charging for Services

● Lunch clubs and transport schemes often charge for services and subsidies may be available from the appropriate statutory service. While charges should be kept to a minimum it may be a false economy to expect volunteers to subsidise the scheme. Many clients are able to contribute and would wish to do so in recognition of the benefits they receive.

> One Day Centre had the majority of its clients funded by Social Services. If one or more clients has to cancel at short notice because of ill health, the money for the clients is not paid. The overheads of the scheme remain the same and it is not possible to find other clients at short notice. Payment is also three months in arrears.

> A community transport scheme has been very grateful to have their minibus maintained and serviced free of charge. Recently the favour has been returned as a relative of one of the mechanics needed a vehicle with a wheel-chair hoist.

PUBLICITY

Some of the most successful schemes have been established more than ten years and they are quick to point out that even now there are local people who claim no knowledge of their existence. The main reason for this is that people are bombarded with information on all sides and filter out those items which are relevant at the time. Big advertising campaigns tempt by frequent repetition, catchy slogans and frequently a tantalising offer. A local voluntary scheme will be unable to go to the same lengths but frequent reminders are worthwhile.

Welcome Packs

Many schemes have been instrumental in producing a welcome pack for new residents. This may encourage newcomers to offer their services as volunteers but most especially aims to incorporate them as members of the community. The pack should include local information about medical and welfare services, churches, sports and leisure, education and youth facilities.

Newcomers Party

In many areas there is a steady turnover of residents; an annual party to welcome newcomers to the community provides a valuable service. Community activities can be advertised and many people will offer time or expertise if approached in a friendly manner and with assurance that they are not entering a lifelong sentence!

Leaflet to every House

This is a good option and can often be included with delivery of some other material such as the local Christmas church service leaflet or parish news. A card or phone sticker would be a good alternative as a reminder.

Posters

Clear bright posters, ideally with a simple logo representing the scheme, should be displayed in public places such as parish and church notice boards, the local surgery, shops, pubs, phone box, bus shelters etc.
These need to be replaced when they become damaged or defaced.

Parish magazines

Free advertisement will often be available and there is usually the opportunity to write regular snippets to keep the scheme in high profile.

Local Newspapers

Press releases of scheme activities, needs and achievements are all most acceptable to a local paper. Take advantage of opportunities which are photogenic as they will make more of an impact on the community.
A letter to the Editor may be productive especially where it highlights a problem which appears to threaten continuation of the scheme.

Local Radio

Requests for equipment and advertising fundraising activities are ideal ways of using local radio.

> One HELPLINE scheme found they had more requests for help after a radio broadcast, but it was not a source of new volunteers.

Word of Mouth

This is the most effective means of publicity and a good scheme will be recommending itself with every job it completes well. It must be associated with attractive publicity material so that when a crisis occurs the client instantly knows who to contact. With every new contact it is worth handing out details of the services offered to remind the client and for handing on to another acquaintance.

Some schemes find it helpful to appoint a publicity officer to use all the opportunities listed above and to create others. The task may be quite small but it needs to be a recognised responsibility. Someone who is unable to help with practical caring may be very willing to take on this role.

SOURCES OF HELP AND ADVICE

Local school / colleges

Students may be available to undertake surveys and provide computer and other skills.

> One scheme used BTEC Business Studies students from a local college to carry out surveys on transport, underage drinking and the need for a Toy Library. This provided valuable experience for the students and the data was well produced and a major stimulus to sources of funding.

Council of Voluntary Service (CVS)

This service tries to coordinate volunteer work throughout the country and where there is a local branch this can be of great assistance. The CVS helps coordination of work with other voluntary organisations and can often provide names of key personnel.

Citizens' Advice Bureau (CAB)

Some clients will need to be referred to the CAB and others may be referred by them to the scheme so a good working relationship is essential. The local CAB will produce an annual report summarising the types of advice which have been requested and this may give valuable insight about the needs of an area.

Rural Community Council or Community Council

These are based in each English county and have a specific remit to assist in community activity. They will provide advice and encouragement, have details of other local schemes, give advice on sources of finance and have direct information about courses or meetings which would be particularly useful. The National Association of Rural Community Councils is ACRE, Somerford Court, Somerford Road, Cirencester, Gloucs GL7 1TW.

Equivalent organisations are :-

- → Wales   - Council for Voluntary Action;
- → Scotland   - Scottish Council for Voluntary Organisations;
- → Northern Ireland - Rural Community Network.

Government Departments - Social Services, Health Authorities Environmental Health

Advice, help and funding may be available from these departments and contact with local officers who know the community will be worthwhile. Some clients may need to be referred to the appropriate professional service.

Health Centres / General Practice

Schemes work within an area served by one or more medical practice. Many doctors and nurses will recognise the benefits of the voluntary care service giving assistance and referring clients.

Ecumenical and Denominational Support

All the main Christian churches proclaim the need for community care but they have very different structures and it is not always easy to know how to approach them. There may be someone such as the local officer for Social Responsibility who has access to much local and national information and can link different groups together for support. Where denominations work together this may come under the county "Churches Together".

Charities

Local charities are often very willing to assist as their constitution may be very specific about the geographic area they are to serve. National charities may provide funding for a project for a specific period. This may enable a scheme to be established and develop other sources of funding and expertise once the charity aid finishes.

The Children's Society has funded a Community Development Worker for three years to work in an area of rural deprivation. She has been able to assist several schemes working closely with local volunteers but providing skill and encouragement and having access to much useful information.

The Midshire Caring Trust

The Midshire Caring Trust supports individuals and organisations involved in caring in the two boroughs of Nuneaton, Bedworth and North Warwickshire. Projects elsewhere can be undertaken when funds permit.

Rural Development Commission

The Rural Development Commission is the Government Agency which works for the wellbeing of the people who live and work in the English countryside. It gives priority assistance to projects in a number of Rural Development Areas, including social projects to encourage community development and help disadvantaged groups.

Arthur Rank Centre

This Churches Rural Resource Centre is a focus for all rural churches and provides support and consultancy to them. Its staff include the Church of England National Rural Officer, the Rural Consultant of the Methodist and United Reformed Churches. The magazine for rural churches "Country Way" is published here.

A Very Personal Note to Christians, our Partners in Care and Possible Funders.

A Message to Christians of Rural Britain.

*I*t is impressive to see how well you integrate your faith with your life in the community and this is to be encouraged. Unselfishness and caring predominate and no one could accuse you of hypocrisy. You may rarely receive thanks from those in authority, but you can be sure that your lives reflect the Christian gospel among those whom you meet. In some areas of the country, Christians have seen the need to develop a more organised system of caring, partly because of changes within the rural populations and also because they have recognised that some people are being neglected. When challenged to look closely at the area where you live, you will see there is more that needs to be done. There is likely to be a building which is central to the community and opening this more widely to the community could be beneficial for all. Your members may possess important skills to assist development of a caring programme and your voices will be influential in speaking for the voiceless. Many of your members are faithful to one denomination, but you will find a new unity in Christ as you work together to love your neighbours. Try to forget your differences and make a conscious effort to invite all the other Christians to work with you. Many who have condemned the churches and chapels for failing to respond to the twentieth century may return to the true faith when they see that it practises what Jesus, the servant king, came to proclaim. Be encouraged to take a small step of faith as many others have done elsewhere and your community will rediscover that a servant church gives, receives and grows in ways beyond understanding.

A Sample Letter to Fundholders / Trusts.

*W*e write to you to ask help in raising the £350 for a new cooker to service the lunch club for elderly in Lower Blodsworth. We have so far raised £180 through local effort and hope that you can now help improve the quality of the service we provide. Our funds are raised by jumble sales, coffee mornings and donations and are used for something essential like an insurance policy or training for our volunteers. Any help you are able to give us enables us to care for those who are disadvantaged in our community and reduces our demands upon the many overstretched government services. We would like to retain our independence and recognise the enormous costs of one visit from a professional from the nearest town.

A Message to the professionals in Social Services, Health Care and others.

*W*e appreciate the vast amount of caring work carried out by the different statutory authorities. Unfortunately many of us have never met you and yet we are all part of a huge body of people who spend some part of our lives caring for others. We are all quick to complain about discrepancies in the system and to point out where others have failed in their duty, but we are all essential in our own way and need to cooperate wherever possible.

One of our greatest assets as volunteers is our knowledge of the local situation. Because we are not part of some state organisation we can sometimes be supportive in a less threatening way. We are also close at hand twenty four hours a day and may be able to provide help that would otherwise require a journey to the nearest town or city. Sometimes we are the eyes, ears and limbs for our community, but we would benefit greatly from a recognition of our service. If we were invited to join you on informative courses, such as "Safe lifting" or "Caring for the confused", this would give us more confidence and we would appreciate the opportunity to meet with you. There must be many situations where we could work together more closely - sometimes you have recognised our work and given funding to support one of our organisers. This has always been a good investment as it has enabled the scheme to develop more quickly and have access to much more useful advice. In fact, these schemes have flourished and now share their skills with neighbouring areas, and will continue to support them until they are established.

A Message to local business.

*W*e know that many of you have had a hard time during the 1990's and it is good to see you have survived as sadly there are many whose businesses remain but memories. Maybe you are new to our area and we want to wish you every success. We love and care for our local community, for those whose families have been here for many generations, but also those who have joined us more recently especially any who are disadvantaged for some reason. You may be aware of our efforts to support one another and to do this we often need skills or access to equipment, fairly low-cost items such as a fridge, cooker, or basic financial assistance. We are really grateful for any help we receive, as we give our time and talents for nothing; but we can often be frustrated or rendered useless when something quite small prevents us giving our best. Please will you look upon us favourably as an important asset to this community and if we approach you with a simple request, help us to discover you too are concerned for those for whom this is home.